# The Beating Heart

Born and raised in Rome, Denise O'Hagan lived in London before emigrating to Sydney, where she lives with her husband and sons. She has a background in commercial book publishing, works as an editor with independent authors through her own imprint Black Quill Press, and is Poetry Editor (Australia/New Zealand) for Irish literary journal *The Blue Nib*. Her poetry is published widely, including in *Eureka Street*, *Literary Yard*, *Other Terrain Journal*, *Backstory Journal*, *The Ekphrastic Review*, *New Reader Magazine*, *Miletus International Literature Magazine* and *Scarlet Leaf Review*. She won First Prize in the Adelaide Plains Poetry Competition and was shortlisted in the Australian Catholic University Poetry Prize, the National Writing Competition, the Robert Graves Poetry Prize and Saolta Arts Poetry Competition. She was also a finalist in the inaugural Institute of Professional Editors' Rosanne Fitzgibbon Editorial Award for her work on the historical novel *Jerome & His Women*.

Website: https://denise-ohagan.com/

Denise O'Hagan
# The Beating Heart

To my father, who bequeathed to me, among other things,
a love of poetry.


'Where does spirit live? Inside or outside
Things remembered, made things, things unmade?'
Seamus Heaney




*The Beating Heart*
ISBN 978 1 76041 928 8
Copyright © text Denise O'Hagan 2020

First published 2020 by
**Ginninderra Press**
PO Box 3461 Port Adelaide 5015
www.ginninderrapress.com.au

# Contents

| | |
|---|---|
| Foreword | 7 |
| Before the party | 9 |
| What was | 10 |
| The lady on the steps | 11 |
| Pine nuts at lunchtime | 13 |
| The flick of a lizard's tail | 14 |
| And the nuns wore lipstick | 15 |
| Fifty-five days | 17 |
| For my cousin in Faenza | 19 |
| A gift for the taking | 21 |
| A stain the shape of Italy | 22 |
| Oblique angles | 24 |
| Mary, Mary, quite contrary | 27 |
| Destination nowhere | 29 |
| I left suitcases | 31 |
| Bedsitter | 33 |
| Lost in transition | 35 |
| I don't want to go back | 36 |
| Honolulu breakfasts | 37 |
| Someone else's morning | 39 |
| Matters of the heart | 41 |
| Old man's eyes | 43 |
| Vermeer in Boston | 44 |
| Boston Uncommon | 46 |
| Charlie | 48 |
| Acquiescence | 50 |
| No room for tears | 51 |
| Between beauty and decadence | 52 |
| The beating heart | 53 |

| | |
|---|---:|
| A journey of sorts | 55 |
| Black box | 57 |
| Now he is here | 59 |
| Recalling Sarah | 61 |
| Blessed to be here | 64 |
| The passing of things | 67 |
| Separateness | 69 |
| A glut of words | 71 |
| Be-mused | 72 |
| In defence of the slimmest of events | 74 |
| My tapestry | 76 |
| 'Burmese, past unknown' | 77 |
| Prayer stool | 79 |
| Spectre | 81 |
| Ficus macrophylla | 82 |
| Election Special | 83 |
| Last stop | 84 |
| The quiet assimilators | 85 |
| In the shadows | 87 |
| | |
| Acknowledgements | 89 |

# Foreword

Infused with heart from its first delicate opening poem, this magnificent debut poetry collection from seasoned wordsmith Denise O'Hagan is an elegant interplay of evocative forays between her internal and external worlds. There is an urgent stillness to much of this work, drawing the reader in with its tenderness towards every aspect of the experience of living. Rich with the colourful cadences of her childhood in Italy, the poet's language pulses with vital, at times visceral, imagery.

Each detail, every moment, no matter how small, is interwoven with meaning, with a reverence often bordering the sacramental. The everyday act of brewing and pouring a morning coffee is elevated to the mystic as 'the imprint of half a century of pourings' materialises 'a fluttering of uneven ghosts'. Wisdom and symbolism abound in this bountiful collection, where 'there is meaning in the fall of a sparrow' and a discarded prayer stool morphs into a Catholic inquisition.

There is melody and whimsy and wry humour ('And the nuns wore lipstick') hiding between darker truths as the poet reveals her unwavering compassion, particularly towards the most vulnerable ('Charlie' and 'Boston Uncommon'). She does not baulk at recording the routine horror of life in Italy during her growing up years – 'the violence that edged things, bomb scares, corruption, political abduction'. This contrasts starkly with the vividly colourful romanticism of her childhood reminiscences where scavenged pine nuts are 'sweeter than any pricey packaged import'.

Though wistful memoir in parts, the poet is never overtly sentimental. Dextrous juxtapositions are everywhere, as are the poet's keen powers of observation. The first blush of maternal love nestles alongside a shocking diagnosis, 'the distorted chambers of your small heart' and 'the awkwardness of visitors'. The poet artfully balances poignant delvings into family and ancestral history with a stripping away of polite society's silky underskirts to reveal a sour underbelly where a 'coiffured housewife with sherry breath risks losing her balance' and 'razor-thin lines' thread the wrists of a gift-laden private schoolgirl.

Like 'a latter-day suburban witch', the poet conjures enchantment throughout this splendid collection – from 'the silver turning of a leaf in the damp air' to 'the throwaway gift of a fallen petal'. This is a poised and polished entrée from an experienced hand. I have no doubt we will see much more of her gifted poetry in the coming years.

Anne Casey, poet<br>Sydney, 2020

# Before the party

It must have just stopped raining
When we arrived. The road, licked for hours
By the quiet slap of countless passing tyres,
Gleamed blackly under the street lamps
Like wet liquorice. We sat for a moment
Watching the mist descend
Cobwebbing the edges of trees and hedges,
The silver turning of a leaf in the damp air,
And the tenting of the telegraph wires
Carrying beads of water like fairy lights
Backlit by the moon.

Feeling privileged to witness
This heady scene, we realised
(As car doors slammed and gravel crunched)
That our reason for having driven here
Was, for a moment, quite forgotten.

# What was

In the kitchen I stand
Tracksuit-clad and blinking
As the click of the front door shuts
The sounds of the day away.

I snuff the gas
And the subterranean gurgling fades to naught
As, like a latter-day suburban witch
Leaning over her latter-day potion
I raise the lid of my coffee pot
Damp my fingers in the steam
And enact the tripart ritual:
Close, lift, and ever so gently pour
A rich and gleaming rope
Of boiling black memoried liquid
Bearing the imprint of half a century of pourings
Into my cup.

Reverently I raise it to my lips
And drink of another old high-ceilinged kitchen
Zigzagged by light cutting in through the shutters
Half-closed against the sun from the run-around balcony
With its fluttering of uneven ghosts on the line
Which spoke of countless bendings and stretchings
As our mothers down the generations casually
Pegged our lives out there on the washing line:
All this inherent in that single sip.

I dip my toast in coffee, smile
And, fortified, swallow away nostalgia
And am, for now, grateful for what was.

# The lady on the steps

Even when I tried not to
I'd catch sight of her on Sunday morning
As, hand cupped in my father's larger one,
We made our way down the narrow street
To the flower stall on the edge of the piazza
And having seen her, I could not un-see her
So I twisted my head back for more
While he ferreted out his pocketed coins
For my mother's bunch of roses:
'Careful now,' he'd always say,
'Hold them by the newspaper, here.'

But more often than not
I'd grip those stems so tight,
My clammy palm imprinted,
Because she'd be sitting there
In her chair outside the palazzo
At the top of a flight of ashen steps
Bolt upright, hands joined in silent supplication
Formally clad, hair pinned and piled high
Haughty, not an ounce of self-pity on her
And her head just kept turning
And turning, back and forth
Forth and back
Back and
Forth.

I was intrigued, frightened
And intrigued by being frightened
I knew not to stare, but did anyway
As in answer to the question I didn't ask,
'Things happen,' my father shrugged.

And in that moment
My childish world quivered and tilted
Its ballast of certainty loosened
And it veered off-course slightly,
Brushed by cool, adult intimations.

# Pine nuts at lunchtime

It was in the way of things
That a casual sighting in a supermarket trolley
In front of me of a packet of nuts
And I was a girl again
Delighting in that lunch hour of freedom
From sitting straight-backed, blank-eyed
At conjugations, calculations or grammatical explanations
Watching our teacher's hand slowly scrape
That white stub of chalk across the blackboard
And wincing as it chanced to squeak.

But when the bell sounded our release, we hurried
Out under the wobbling shade of the umbrella pines
And ran and dodged and hid and found until
Flushed and gasping, we came to rest.
We knew how to spot them then
Those slight charcoal-coloured oblongs
Of pine nuts nestled in the grooves of crazy paving
Like they had been dipped in ash.

Slipping off a shoe, heel in hand we'd kneel
And with the deft turn of a schoolgirl's wrist
We would smash them open, but gently
So as not to injure the pale, delicate-tasting flesh inside
Fresh to the world, and sweeter
Than any pricey, packaged import.

# The flick of a lizard's tail

Salmon-coloured, two-storeyed villa
Like a giant terracotta pot
Burnt in the sun:
This was my first school.

But memory is a fickle beast.
It's not our teachers' faces,
Far less their lessons, that linger
But the flick of a lizard's tail at recess
In the shell-encrusted flowerpot
Behind grand columns of ivy
On crazy paving.

Or the dark bruise of foliage
At the end of the playground
Into which we'd dash
At the ringing of the bell
To play the games all children play
And hide our own confusions.

Or the impatient crunch of gravel underfoot
As we waited for the bus to take us home
Past those familiar ancient paving stones
Straight as the ruler we used in maths
Brushed by grass, shadowed by pines
And heavily layered in history
But which, to me, was simply
The place I found
My pet snail.

# And the nuns wore lipstick

On occasion
We used to holiday
In the small towns of northern Italy
Or drive further north, across the border
To Switzerland, which
To my childish eyes
Glistened, gleamed, and looked so prosperous.

All was new and neat and tidy
Even the leaves seemed to fall tidily
From boxes of optimistic flowers
Beneath the windowsills.
Such persistent cheerfulness
Left me nervous
I must admit.

Everything was accounted for,
No loose ends, no unclaimed parts,
Cuckoo clocks and countless watches ran to time.
(No bomb scares, no gypsies, no beggars)
So we strolled through mountain villages,
Sipped hot chocolate in pretty cafés,
Climbed into chairlifts,
(My mother's desultory step
Not quite in keeping
With those of eager tourists).

Once, we passed a group of nuns
And my father shook his head.
'Did you see that?' as his pace slowed.
'They're wearing lipstick!'
The disbelief, the quiet horror in his voice
Stayed with me long after
The other images receded like slides,
And took up their ordered places
As mementos of a distant time.

# Fifty-five days

We shrugged at bomb scares at school
Locked our doors, watched our bags and our steps
And skirted any lone bag on a bench.
These were the years of lead, after all:
The violence that edged things was rising
And life was getting a ragged quality to it.
The heart was falling out of the city
Its famous walls bulged with sanctioned corruption
Handshakes and deals that never happened.

So when a famous politician was kidnapped
And held hostage for fifty-five days,
We'd run out of shock, so to speak.
Yet his heavy-lidded resignation dragged at our hearts
As a mugshot released grainy proof that he was, still, alive
And his letters of appeal went public.
'In truth,' he wrote, 'I feel a little abandoned…'

The government, curiously, was implacable:
Its refusal – this time! – to negotiate for one of their own
Was cold and hard as marble.
Not the supplications of family and friends
Nor the offer of papal intervention
Stemmed the inevitable, blossoming horror.

To the wail of sirens and a thickening crowd
His bloody, bullet-studded body was found
Chained and crumpled in the boot of a Renault
And dumped in the centre of Rome.
The symbolism was callously clear:
A sacrifice had been laid at a political altar
But by whom?

Then was the time of recriminations and allegations
Of tip-offs unfollowed and other inexplicable revelations
Strikes, demonstrations, and calls for resignations
Spawning ever more accusations
Which clung like mist to the men in black suits
And shadowed the stretching of the years ahead.

In 1978, the leader of the ruling Christian Democrats, Aldo Moro, was kidnapped and murdered in Rome by the Red Brigades. His 'historic compromise' would have been the first Communist representation in a Western European government.

# For my cousin in Faenza

The hollow of time
That hangs between Christmas and New Year
Found the four of us
Bound (was it really on a whim?)
For Faenza,
That city of arches, mist and gloom
And, of course, ceramics,
So startlingly and exquisitely colourful
They hardly seemed to fit in at all.

Those days
Indistinct, hazy, blurring at the edges
Form part of the landscape of my mind
Its contours indistinguishable
From my remembered version of it:
The muted beauty
Of roads dotted by the tips of cypresses
Walks through Renaissance colonnades
And furtive late-night liquors
Sipped while the city slumbered
And we fed on laughter and conversation.

How to understand
What we felt then?
Faenza,
(Surely the city merits its own line)
Or Faventia, as the ancient Romans knew it
With its Etruscan, even Celtic origins,
Was elegant, contained and onomatopoeic.

You could not hurry in winter in Faenza
Time was slowed to a point of utter stillness
And transposed to this foggy alternative reality
We could, at last, breathe free.
I realise now, though I didn't then,
That we were all escaping something
If only a certain disjointedness in our normalcy
A lack of pieces fitting snugly together
Even me, sensing as only the young can do
That primitive, universal lunge towards
Inhibition.

We were always going to return,
Our journey by train as nebulous as the fog itself,
Yet we were fortified, buttressed against what lay ahead
And something had, to a degree,
Shifted.

# A gift for the taking

Hunched on the edge of her bed
Fingernail curling into the blanket
She felt the slow wings of panic
Closing in around her
Beating her thoughts out of her
Squeezing her breath thread-thin.

*Life is a gift, my father said*

She sat there
A husk of her former sixteen-year old self
So light she could blow away
It would be a relief, really.

*It's a gift I never asked for, I replied*

But what would it be like
To not be?

*No one asked, he responded*

Hugging her thin T-shirt tighter
She frowned at the ink stain on her sleeve
And shivered on the edge
Of a perilous moment.

*It's still a gift for the taking.*

So she clutched at his words
Mantra-like, embossing them
On the walls of her mind
Shielding herself
From herself
And from what lay outside.

# A stain the shape of Italy

It's when I least expect it
Stilled in a queue, perhaps,
Or stalled at traffic lights,
That the fingers of my memory
Pick at the past
Loosening the scabs of memory:
It's irresistible.

One little prod
And the present flakes away
As I'm clutching my mother's hand again
Down the cobblestoned short-cut side street
Softened by the tread of centuries
To where her dressmaker lived;
Or recoiling at the garish wallpaper
In a rented room in a house for foreign students
With swirls and whorls on green and cream
And a stain the shape of Italy
Which made me homesick;
Or wincing at the bulge of vein in my father's temple
As suited and tied and elegant one last time
He strains up the sloping steps of St Canice's
To see his grandson, his own father's namesake,
Live to be baptised.

That these milestones of our lives
(Laboriously recounted, photographed,
Or documented in countless other forms)
Are glued together by such details
We scarcely realise until later
When they emerge with doubled force
From the backrooms of our memory
Where, pasted in by the years,
They had lain dormant, waiting
For a moment such as this.

# Oblique angles

The geometry of our lives
Can be carved out neatly and solidly
Steadily, even stolidly
Or set at oblique angles
Which makes them
Riskier, more startling
And more brittle.

You see them sometimes
The privileged, displaced set
Busily leisured, multi-holidayed, expats
Marked out by exemptions and immunities
Inhabiting a wider radius
Than those around them.
'Are you in the foreign office?'
'Or the diplomatic service?'
They handle speculation easily
They're used to it
But really
It hardly matters
Where they came from
Or where they're going.

And so the women frolic
In Europe's playgrounds
With plump purses
And thickening waistlines
Do art classes
To catch up on culture
Ostensibly
While their far-flung husbands
Unfasten leather briefcases
Delve the pockets of their other lives,
And their children
Are in Saint this
Or International that
Take your pick
Of which language,
And the maid
Who comes on Fridays
Dusts the dining room desultorily
And pockets a coin on the floor.

Yet the coiffured housewife
Who packs her children's lunch
And takes them to the bus stop
With a sherry breath
Risks losing her balance
And totters home
Alone.

And her husband
Boarding his flight home
Thinks of the woman he just left
Her sad accusing eyes,
Hopes she won't try to ring him
And marvels
At the heavy ramifications
Of choices made
On a whim.

# Mary, Mary, quite contrary

Mary, Mary, quite contrary
When did it all go wrong?

Was it your expensive schools
With their expansive rules
Where your antics got you expelled?

Or the summer holidays abroad
From which you returned
Smiling and taut
Razor-thin lines threading your wrists
And gifts in your hands?

Or your determined immersion
Into a cold hard foreign city
A baptism of adulthood, of sorts,
Among flinty, unforgiving crowds
Jostling for the same jobs
And your too-eager embracing of people
Who used you and bruised you and left you alone?

Or the aching need for intimacy
Sewn in infancy by a mother who left you
Packed her bags and a one-way ticket
To a brand-new life far away
And later shunned your tentative advances?

Whatever it was, the last time I saw you
You were thinner than you had ever been
Your flat was neater than it had ever been
As if you were halfway to somewhere else
Like your heroine, Sylvia Plath, perhaps
But you left no fanfare or *Bell Jar*
Just empty pill jars
And a father's silent, spilling horror.

Yet still I hold
The pieces of your broken soul
In my heart, with the shards of possibilities
Of the fully fledged person you could have become.
It was all there, my friend, in your defiant blonde stance
And your exuberant giggles of childish complicity
As you stood on the cusp of life:
It just never happened.

# Destination nowhere

We twisted and dipped and dipped again
The road cast over the land like a ribbon
By turns slack over flats and taut over hills
Stretching and curving, rising and falling.
We chased it as children might a rainbow
In thrall to a never-ending journey
Our destination nowhere.

Squinting in the high sun of siesta hour
Against the dull hum of the engine
Lulling our thoughts, blunting our senses
But for a passing pity for the tiny bodies of insects
Smeared across the window screen, then blown off
By pure speed.

A village shrank in our rear-vision mirror
And its outlying shacks, abandoned long ago,
Lay scattered like crumbs on the hillside.
High above us, a monastery ate into sheer rockface,
Granite testimony to faith and structural engineering,
Stalling time and raising the big unanswerables,
Then falling away into the past as the fields filled in again
And swathes of dark-tipped wheat on slender stems
Spread in a single silken undulating carpet.

We didn't talk; we didn't need to.
Poppies cut a line of ketchup red
Across a field; olive trees curled into view
Squat, grey and hunched in on themselves
Gnarled forms of warning and reproof.

We chose to look away
Eschew the music, adjourn the aftermath
And cup the moment in our hands
For a brief eternity.

I hold it still.

# I left suitcases

I left suitcases
in my parents' apartment
with foldings of clothes
pressed smooth as stone
my favourite boots
(wedge heels, wedged in)
worn paperbacks
dedicated and inscribed
commemorations of birthdays and other days
a little wooden Madonna with a cracked base
a soft wad of diaries
letters upon handwritten letters
with their trelliswork
of various handwritings
in various inks
confiding, entrusting
advising and entreating
and my old green stamp album
in short, the fascinatingly random
paraphernalia of adolescence.

I left suitcases
with friends abroad
fully intending
to retrieve them
when I had pulled
the threads of my life
into some semblance of order
but I never did
really do either
my life spun on
I ran to catch up
never imagining I'd be
on the move again.

I left suitcases
with my cousin even further away
the contents of which
was increasingly, obsessively
comprehensive, a cross-section
of a life in miniature
it seems I could barely move
without leaving
compartments of myself
behind
just like
I left suitcases.

# Bedsitter

Strewn throughout this subdivided, many-sided house
Run through by its creaking backbone of a staircase
And several narrow arterial corridors
Are two or three rooms to a floor,
The smaller ones pasted on like afterthoughts,
And one of them is mine.

Narrow as a capsule
More a container of daily necessities than a home
It signifies a pause, a hiatus, nothing more,
A chilly low-cost limbo, a waiting room of sorts,
The place I unravel my nine-to-five secretarial self
Let the feelings of the day unspool
Over a half-eaten leftover takeaway
And yesterday's wine bottle full of emptiness
As downstairs other people's footsteps
Pound the worn, beige wall-to-wall moquette
And the front door clicks the outside world away.

Cocooned in bedsit-land I sit
Forever a foreigner, unnaturally alert,
Yet if I'm still and silent and listen hard enough
I can hear the backward creak of time
Peeling away the plaster of the years,
The makeshift cover-ups and crude add-ons,
And can feel the brush of petticoats,
See the imprint of footsteps hastening downstairs
Past banisters polished creamy as butter,
Wallpapered walls chock-a-block with paintings,

And hear the murmur of confident conversation
Behind panelled, stained-glass doors opening
To a slice of parlour with burgundy walls
And a fireplace flanked by flickering lamps:
The air is rich and heavy with success,
Smug and snug and velvet warm.
A young maid with her tray of empties slips out
Her apron fluttering about her like a ghost,
A bead of perspiration glossy on her forehead.

I tuck the layers of the past back under my belongings
(How paper-thin the present seems!)
Tidy up my thoughts and dishes,
Stand and stretch and wipe my brow
And set my alarm for another six-thirty start.

# Lost in transition

It wasn't the foreign student visas
Applied for and accrued, year after year
Nor the waiting in glassy dusty consulates
(Forms filled out, rubber-stamped and signed)
Or alien queues at airports
(Yes, I know I have to reapply)
Or even the many goodbyes
(Of course I'll write, will you?).

It was a cashier's casual comment
As I laid down my last-minute purchase
(Flying-friendly sneakers on special)
The day before leaving:
'You're not from here, are you?'
While her fingers stabbed the register
That sliced my confidence
So I pretended to mis-hear
(Not wanting to admit
I'd been there ten years).

Perhaps it was the timing of it
But like a bruise that wouldn't fade,
The question lingered, setting in train
The first of many diminutive deceits
And innocuous insincerities
That even now, decades later,
I'm still reeling in my sense of space
To prove my place,
My 'here'.

# I don't want to go back

I don't want to go back
To where I grew up
As a tourist,
Brushing shoulders
With ghosts of family and friends.

My memories are so carefully displayed
In the cabinet of my mind
Selected, positioned,
And polished to a gleam
That the blunt touch of re-experience
Would surely tarnish them.

# Honolulu breakfasts

It is the breakfasts
that stick in my mind
maple syrup light
slashing
through bamboo walls
sloshing
over our pancakes
toast and coffee
as, morning after morning,
(how long a week can seem)
we climbed the wooden stairs
to a rickety corner café
we called our own
gorging ourselves
on blue skies, and
palm trees
swaying and sashaying
like elegant ladies, over
the pale curve of beach
pitted with tourists
in the background
the glitter glare of glass
of luxury hotels
hard, moneyed places
(you could see how
those brochures
came to be written)

and in the evenings
we moved easily
among people
laughing people
as they tequila'd
their time away
so easy to live
as if you
are happy too
sometimes
I even believed
I was.

# Someone else's morning

The sun bores down
On a rectangle of synthetic green:
An inner-city playground.

The empty swing hangs immobile
Its knotted metal chains glinting
Its mottled wooden seat waiting.

It is one of the passed-over places
An oasis of discomfort, cut out from shade
Of the surrounding canopy of trees.

A little boy plays alone
Throwing a twig high into the sky.
It does not come down again.

Under the trees, a man's rough call
Blurry with drink and loneliness
Lingers in the hot air.

Paper bags, like big brown leaves,
Drift stained and empty along the pavement
Shored up by the playground railings.

'Mama, look!' The boy has made a face
Out of sticks, cigarette ends for his eyes.
His delight is palpable.

The young woman in the laneway
Walks across, slowly, each step an effort.
Her arms, so thin, reach out to him.

I cannot stand and watch this, I cannot stay.
I tuck my son into his stroller and turn away.

Written in King's Cross, an inner-city suburb of Sydney where the bohemian lifestyle it is known for lies like the thinnest of blankets over the deeper problems of homelessness, addiction and crime.

# Matters of the heart

I had not realised
Hands and fingers could be so small
So pink and crinkly, nails and all
A little tiny human being
Complete, perfect
Except that you were not
I could not hear
I did not want to know
The complicated diagnosis
They were pressing upon us
I'd never heard of Ebstein's Anomaly
Just wanted to hold you with my eyes
Through the plastic pod of the incubator
Moving so the reflections didn't take away
A single little part of you.

While you lay swathed in lines
Bathed in fluorescent lights
And fed on oxygen
We bit our nails in the waiting room
'A rare condition,' the doctor's careful words
Pronounced at last, oracle-like
Would later pour through our minds
(And we'd sieve them, hungrily
To extract a drop of extra meaning).
'Excuse me? No, severe. Hard to say…'
He paused with professional reticence.
'It's a case of wait and see.'

And so began a chain of days
Of waiting and seeing and waiting yet again
For the distorted chambers of your small heart
Like a microcosm of all imperfect structures
To adapt their functions to the outside world
Become mini-experts at compensation
Minimise the differences, fool the observer
And play the ultimate fit-in game.

Yet I feel it now, and sensed it then
(Seeing the awkwardness of visitors
Unsure of what to say, and how)
That your imperfection mirrors a greater one
In the hearts of all of us around you
Who struggle to acknowledge, much less accept
What we cannot understand or justify.

Ebstein's Anomaly is a rare congenital heart disease affecting one in every 20,000 live births, including my son Isaac.

# Old man's eyes

Your throaty snuffle signals
The start of the familiar night-time ritual
I raise you up, blinking at the clock: 2.15 a.m.
The hour that hangs between night and day
The slow slug of time, creeping, inching, edging.

I settle you against me, watching you
And noticing the little things:
The fluff that nestles in the curves of your fingers,
The vein in your eyelid that trembles when you dream
The blue-grey eyes, old man's eyes
As if you already knew what was in store.

But perhaps this is a mother's exhaustion talking –
You're still a baby, after all.

# Vermeer in Boston

I'd waited decades
To see that knowing glance, forever paused
That letter being permanently written
And that ermine-edged yellow morning jacket.

Yet I found myself, ridiculously,
In the exhibition by accident
Travelled half the world here
For another reason entirely
And stood, clammy palmed and weary
My thoughts haywire, clinging
To another imagined room a mere walk away
Where a team of specialists
Pored over our son
Whose opened chest
Was spread like a canvas
For the surgeons to splatter and daub
And create another version
Of his deformed and failing heart:
Their masterpiece.

And while all this was happening
I met her painted gaze, unflinching,
Wondering, even then, what she'd been writing
(And to whom, and why).
She'd raised her eyes, unblinking
Poised and faintly mocking
Too intelligent, I couldn't help thinking,
For twenty-first century positivity.
Instead, her Mona Lisa almost-smile
Stayed with me almost all the while

I waited for the phone call
I didn't feel alone.

And when they'd finished
Eleven long hours later
Applied the appropriate solutions
Brushed away the bloody residue
Hung up their paintbrushes,
It came:
'Your son is in recovery.'

Still later, on the long flight home,
Juggling pills and international time differences
Her enigmatic expression flew with me
Long after the shadows around her faded
With her writing box and ink-wells,
Her slim stilled quill pen,
The satin ribbons shining in her hair
And the round of her wrist bone
All this slipped away –
Until I saw it later
In a catalogue.

And in one moment
I was back in Boston with her,
Waiting.

Written after waiting for news of our son's open-heart surgery in Boston Children's Hospital, November 2015. Coincidentally, the nearby Museum of Fine Arts was holding an exhibition on the painters of the Dutch Republic, which included Vermeer's *A Lady Writing*.

# Boston Uncommon

Over the grills in Boston Common
As the evening turns to night
Dark figures drift into view
Warming themselves in belches of steam
That arise, as groggy and insubstantial
As vapours from Hell.

Hoarse cries, red-rimmed eyes
Gloves clutching at brown paper bags
Like holy relics.
Ignoring the averted eyes
And the judicious stepping aside
Of the lacquered mainstream
These misfits of society, these malcontents
Blot out their demons and
Soak away their lives
In alcohol.

The last commuter has long since gone
When these lumped, slumped figures
Alternative versions of our darker selves
Subdued at last, lie down
Blanketed, beanied and scarved
Arms crossed over, heads bowed
Wrapped in plastic like giant plasters
Suturing the city's most intimate wounds.

A trolley ride away
In the salubrious salons of the well-to-do
Where money and class work hand in glove
The high court judge, the stockbroker and the policymaker
Uncoil themselves from their cases, spreadsheets and drafts
And tend, at last, to their own needs.
Drunk on pride and vintage sherry
They lick their lips, lock their doors
Flick off their chandeliers
Pad across mahogany floors
To retire at last to bed
And (with the help of a pill, perhaps)
To a clear, untroubled sleep.

# Charlie

Every hospital has a Charlie
Someone who's slipped through society's cracks
And sits obstinately on the outside
A grit in the eye of every passerby
And a reproof to government healthcare.

He was sitting there today
By the thick glass sliding doors
A great raw trunk of a man
Marooned in his chair
By bewilderment and swollen ankles,
A latter-day Humpty-Dumpty.

His eyes rake you in as you walk past
Slit windows to a private hell
As he wages his daily battle with self-expression
But his sentences dangle, words mangled
Limp as the cigarette in his mouth.

You nod and smile:
It's the least you can do
Hoping this tiniest of overtures
Won't lead to more
Then wishing you didn't feel that way
Because you know, deep down,
Irrelevance plays no part in it –
There is meaning in the fall of a sparrow
And Charlie has something to tell us.

So you plug up the holes in your heart
With well-practised, comforting pity,
Blink away the tears in his eyes
And wave goodbye to something in yourself
As you walk on to the rest of your life
Scarcely daring to wonder
If things had been different
Could you have been him?

## Acquiescence

I've no sooner squeezed the buzzer
When the doors slide soundlessly open
And I'm absorbed into the foyer's beige anonymity
Fumbling my hoard of little disallowed things
Into the unyielding steel-grey locker
Sealing it with the same code I always use
(I cling to old habits like a child to a blanket)
As a second set of doors swing open
And she nods with a professional smile –
It's her again, I recognise the tip of tattoo at her neck
(My husband would frown, but it amuses me)
And I'm led back inside again
Following the pad of rubber-soled shoes, dutifully
Keeping my thoughts in line, prudently
Down pastel-coloured corridors, screamingly peaceful
Right, left, then we take another right
There's a rhythm to it, a cool cadence
My shoulders loosen, and I match my step
To the clink of keys on the chain at her side
And we round the curve of the main desk
Sitting like a giant capsule among a constellation of rooms
(Repository of remedies for unimaginable maladies
And dispenser of medication for every trepidation)
The mere sight of which somehow
Smooths the ruffled corners of my mind
Lulling into reluctant acquiescence
Its tangled thoughts and murky hopes.

I walk on to Room 17, at the far end
(Unlucky where I grew up, I'm uneasily aware)
And ask my son, 'How are you doing today?'

# No room for tears

His fingers moved swiftly
Folding, smoothing and folding again
Until every plane sat snug against the next
*'Fold flap down along centre crease'*:
The dotted lines and arrows of instruction
Brought to textured, exuberant life
To the wonderment of patients around him.

But deep inside he carried
The hard bullet of conviction
That this was no hobby.
He wasn't just making boxes or flowers or birds
But smoothing out the creases of life
Pressing out the awkward bits
Filling each space with meaning
And pure targeted purpose
Shiny and inviolable.

Climbing into the world
Of geometrical precision
And cleanly calculated precepts
Absolved him from ambiguity
Dismissed damning doubt
And left no room for tears.

## Between beauty and decadence

Like a shred of satin
Crumpled and creamy
It caught my eye
Lying there, near a clothes peg
Against the brick red patio.

Luminous, exposed
Halfway between beauty and decadence
With the day's bruise already on it:
The world's aches
Perfectly expressed
In the throwaway gift
Of a fallen petal.

# The beating heart

The quick-fire rhythm of her typewriter keys
Then the carriage return, like a sharp intake of breath
(The kitchen table was my mother's desk)
As characters took shape and situations emerged
('Would he do that? Is this what she'd really say?')
And the pile of typescript pages grew with her excitement
Alongside their ghostly replicas, the carbon copies,
Weighted down by chunky glass ashtrays: pure energy.

Later, papers spread about his desk
My father's glasses catch the light as he stretches
('How long till dinner?'),
Then bends again, dark head inclined
Over sloping handwriting, crossings out,
A swirl of pencils, biros, a half-empty whiskey glass
And a rubbish bin crumpled high with drafts
Grappling third-world food shortages.
It was a calmer, more cloistered atmosphere
In the study lined with books, with doors of panelled glass.

This, then, was writing as I knew it.
And my friends and I mimicked them
With our own childish fabrications
Hammered out on summer afternoons
On a second-hand portable typewriter
So they would look 'real'.

Even now, decades later, it seems
Direct experience is not enough:
I was ever wrapped in words, and
Rapt in the worlds they made,
Still feel the tug to describe, distill,
And dare, with pen and paper,
To move the boundaries of what's real
And write a world into existence,
People it with those who may have lived
Or did or could or should have
And give voice to the maybe-souls
Who inhabit the fringes of our subconscious.

And when we touch the pulse, the raw emotion,
Of the deep-seated, nameless thoughts and feelings
Which move us all, then we are touching
The beating heart of poetry itself.

# A journey of sorts

You didn't see me
But I turned back
And then for years
Every time I passed that place
I'd see your crumpled form
Wheelchaired across the courtyard
Plastic bracelet pale against your wrist,
Resistance in the set of your shoulders.

Did a lifetime spent abroad
Sliced up between three continents
And all the years of travel
(Good luck tiki in your inner pocket)
With their attendant rituals
Of collars pressed and briefcases clicking
Inching forwards in countless check-in queues
Nodding acceptance of clunky hotel keys
Patient layers of rewritten drafts
Pencilled scribbles up and down the margin
Handshakes, boardrooms, coffee in plastic cups
Inhaling overblown officialdom
With cigarettes over too-long lunches
In that quiet way of yours – did all this
Stand you in good stead?
For this, too, was a journey of sorts.

The white gash of your hospital gown
The glow of multicoloured monitors
Recording your vital functions
While nurses replenished, adjusted and tweaked
The spaghetti curls of drip lines and silver stands
With which my mother and I did hopeless battle
To ease your situation
Prompting a final, wry quip
And a chuckle from a nurse of stone:
Humour *in extremis*.

And on the last night
They gave you the last rites
And then we settled down
To wait.

# Black box

Yesterday I found
A small lacquered box
Which had sat on her dresser
Since I remember.
As blackly shiny now as then
The painted bird's eternal flight
Towards scattered painted petals
A constant, unwavering thing
In a wavering world.

I know what's in it
And feel the thrill of familiarity
When I lift the lid
On a little piece of the past
And hold again
The Paris corner café matchbox
Delicately illustrated, and holding in turn,
My miniature father cut-out in sepia
Younger, more vulnerable than I ever knew him,
And underneath, a printed Roman Society library card
With several other cards from other libraries,
The stub of a borrower's docket
(She was ever a reader, my mother)
A hairpin, iron-grey and bobbled at the ends
Such as she used to use and are used no longer.

And at last, there she is herself
Arresting and poised in black and white
Pointy dark-rimmed sunglasses in hand,
Her head turned back to look at me
One fine eyebrow arched
Her eyes holding mine
Through the years.

# Now he is here

I tread between slabs of stone
shining like the underbellies of giant bugs
in the shimmering light
of an autumn afternoon
and think that this was just
the sort of day he would have loved.

He used to eat olives
and anchovies
and sardines
and now he is here.

He used to drink
his coffee espresso
standing up
at a bar
and now he is
here.

He was
a quiet man
a reserved man
who guarded
his feelings carefully
he did not subscribe
to the confessional age
but rather
to an older European formality
like his suits
his polished shoes

and his ability
to listen
and now he
is
here.

I jam the bottlebrush
into granite urns
spots of blood
speckling my knuckles
and now
he
is
here.

# Recalling Sarah

I'm moved to write to you
Whom I have never known
Whom I have always known.

How can it be? I am puzzled
By my own assurance
(I, who am assured about so little)
Over someone who died
Before I was born
And lived a world away.

I look at my creased, handed-down photo
Of your softly sepia'd twenty-year-old self
And wonder.
Your dark-eyed composure
Composes in turn my thoughts
There's poise in your posture
And challenge in the tilt of your head
A delicate sense of expectancy
As you look back through me and beyond
Towards a future that never really happened.

The parameters of disease
Marked out in the white-sheeted hospital bed
The tread of nurses, the clink of medicine bottles
And their hopeless ministrations, all this
A mere decade away.

For now, though
You're all dressed up, bridal-like again
And oh, so elegant
A photo was no small occasion, then.
But in your eyes
(My father's eyes, my eyes)
Is a foreshadowing
Of space where
A life should have been.

When you coughed
Strawberry splashes
Through your handkerchief,
And sweated the night away
Awaking fatigued and heavy-lunged,
They knew.

You wept, as they took you away
The corridors of your memory
Running you back to when
You held your child's heartbeat close to yours
Not covered up, separated, segregated
Portioned off like something unclean.

And when they brought your son to visit
The nurses bit their lips
And kept him at a distance.
It was a cruel farewell.

I think
He never stopped missing you
And the missingness
Was passed down, and down.

And so your photo
Still sits in front of me
A haunting, present absence.

My grandmother passed away from pulmonary tuberculosis
in 1932 in Te Kuiti, New Zealand. She was 32.

# Blessed to be here

'Europeans who decided to make a new home in New Zealand
embarked on the longest journey of migration in human history.'
(*TeAra, Encyclopaedia of NZ*)

Our journeys make us, they say, they define us
And to an extent, they are us.

It was a hard voyage
And at twenty-six, he was a hard man
Leaving the rugged squiggle of coastline
That was Ireland, and all he knew,
With a wife and young sons in tow
Bound for the other side of the world
And who knew how many long months at sea
Cramped into the tired, tiered bunks in steerage
Down below deck with the vermin and the seepage
And the cargo and other government immigrants
Pushing and shoving and jostling and squabbling,
The filth was palpable, the stench near tangible
And privacy was just a word
There, where tedium vied with fear
(Shall we play quoits or pray for mercy?)
To the continuous churning of the sea
The incessant grinding of wood on wood
And squelching and squeaking of slippery planks
Waves slapping and slopping the deck
And froth dribbling like unmopped spittle.

He wondered sometimes whether they'd make it
While his wife complained about washing in a teacup,
The potatoes and too-salty meat that never ran out.
'And not enough greens,' she said, 'Never enough greens.'
'Hold your tongue, woman,' he told her.
'We're blessed to be here, and don't you forget it.'

She turned away from him then,
And didn't turn back
Until the day their infant son
Coughed his life away in her arms
And he gently prised his small body away
From the ship doctor's brandied breath,
His rough farmer's hands shaking,
Saw to it that he was wrapped in sackcloth
Like the other little ones before him
Weighted and slipped overboard
With muttered prayers and gritted teeth
And barely a splash.

No desire for recrimination, nor inclination
Too stricken for tears or lamentation,
He and his wife stood hand in hand and side by side,
Watching the silk smooth water,
The water that now held their son.

The trajectory of his life
Was set in his jaw then:
He had his life to make.
He was going to survive
For his wife, his son
By God, he was going to survive.

Inspired by my great-great-grandfather's voyage from famine-stricken Ireland to New Zealand in April 1865.

# The passing of things

I slip off my shoes and sit down
With a good five minutes to spare,
My eyes on the hands of the clock
As they drag their slow way round.

The minutes are heavy.

I have always been
Fascinated with time,
This notion
That we can partition up
And measure
The passing of things,
Put a line like a child's ruler
Between past and future
Whereas in fact
The transition from
Now to then is indefinable
In the very act of grasping it
It is already gone
If it ever existed at all.

Perhaps this is why
I am drawn
To memories
Recordings, reminiscing
And all manner of traces
Like my photograph album
Obsessively arranged
As if in that arranging

I could superimpose
An order
Or clarity
Perhaps even a meaning
That may never
Have been there
When then
Was
Now.

# Separateness

The silence
Between us
Thickens and grows
And flows around us
Like a third presence
Waiting, malevolently,
For one of us to break it.

How did we
Get to this point?
Is there a line running
From the quickened heartbeat
The clutched hand
Of youth
And easy collusion
Of middle age
To this?
Was the end
Implicit in the beginning?
Or did we
Take a wrong turn
Creating a fault line
Damaging ourselves
And dislocating the 'us'?
My thoughts are heavy, clunky
And going nowhere.

Years of misalignment
Have made us wary
Suspicion lies coiled
Between us, serpent-like,
So we take refuge in routine,
Imbibing the evening news
With our chamomile tea
And the other rituals
Of stale, safe domesticity.

But all the while
Nuggets of resentment
Weigh down any deeper disclosure
And neither of us
Want to admit
To boredom.

# A glut of words

On any given day
There is a glut of words around me
On doorways, streets and signs
Informing, instructing, warning
On labels, shops and cars
Coaxing, cajoling, luring
In restaurants and bars
The many-tentacled monster
Of modern communication
Pressing in around me,
Assertive and insistent
Audacious and capricious
Oppressing and compressing me
Sometimes, they almost make me choke.

But then there are others
The passed over or forgotten words
Scrawled on beggars' placards
The bewildered words
Whispered away in the slipstream of time
Crumpled thoughts in a lover's thrown-away note
Fragments of people's conversations
Caught in the wind on a street corner.

Must it be like this?
Words should be held like little gems
Precious-like
In the soft cup of a child's hand
And picked out tenderly, one by one
So we can slip into the lining of situations
And see them from the inside.

# Be-mused

Poetry turns on a pause
In a champagne conversation,
Flickers into being in the space
Between the starter and the main course,
And glides you through
Satin silences.

And when you get home
You try to write it down
You fidget and frown
Refuse to give up
Start to get angry
And then you realise,
Hitting the dead end of concentration,
That those squirls you've made
Even the doodles
Snaking towards the margin
Are taking you somewhere:
They're luminous,
And those hesitant hieroglyphics
Scraped out by your biro
Against a pale page
Are numinous,
Slowing you down
Until you can see
The shape of your sentences
Rise above their own meaning,
Opening you up
To the music behind
What's said.

It's not the clink of crystal
At the cocktail party
Nor the silken conversation
Between black suits or pearled dresses,
It's in the ensuing fold of stillness
Where poetry
Arises.

# In defence of the slimmest of events

I shuffle papers, pick up my pen,
Unsure of where to start, and why
Everything's a subject, and the slightest matter
Is what seems to me to matter most:
A note of music, a falling leaf, a child's fluting cry
All are prompts to a world without
Or resonate with one within.

'But surely,' a little devil whispers,
'You can do better than this?
In such a slim event, barely an event at all,
Who on earth would take an interest?
Surely you need a grander, more complicated theme,
At the very least, something slightly controversial
To catch the readers' eye, bait them,
And reel in their dwindling attention spans!
You could elaborate, reference and allude –
At any rate, you must impress.'

I waver, succumb a moment, then rouse myself.
No, I will not be lured by others' expectations
Tailoring my subject, adjusting my style
To humour those whom I don't know
And court the nod of the establishment
With its attendant prizes for verses
Weighed down by literary conceit
Laden with allusions and laced with Latin.

Must we prop up our lines like this
Lending legitimacy to our writing
Give evidence of our wider reading
And strut our credentials?
We need, first and last,
Quite simply,
To feel.

# My tapestry

Over how many ways with words
And turns of phrase, and scribbles and scrawls
Have my fingers lingered?

In getting a feeling
For the spirit that moves
The outward, literal, form
We step into the writer's mind
To follow the contours of their thoughts,
Only then can we dare
To shape their material
Reinforcing the fabric of expressions
Trimming away the frills, removing padding
And shreds of ambiguity folded into phrases
Stretching sentences until they're taut with meaning
One following on one from another
Until they all hang perfectly, pleasingly
With no loose threads,
Seamless.

For we editors are tailors,
(Seamstresses of old
Working in the back rooms of history,
Heads bowed, diligently, invisibly)
We cut and paste and nip and tuck,
Sewing it all together
Until the point is clear.

Here, at this work,
My pen's my needle.
I stitch in words:
This is my tapestry.

## 'Burmese, past unknown'

Plump and poised, you stretch and yawn
Arch your back and, circling, settle down
Into the warmed, blanketed groove
Of my crumpled, rumpled unmade bed
And survey me.

I daily marvel at your confidence
Which budded and grew
In the cool dark space
Beneath my bed, where no one
Could get at you.

Weeks on the streets had
Hollowed your stomach
Grubbied and matted your coat
Crusted your nose, and
Traced ridges of bones in your fur.

All these indignities and more,
They couldn't wash out of you
In the cat shelter where,
Wary of contact, withdrawn and forlorn,
You hunched in on yourself.

Yet when they opened the door
You turned your eyes to us
And they were green
I thought of marbles
Black-outlined, Egyptian-like.

All this over a year ago now
You are the same, but not.
Your slender tail says it all
Swirling, curling
A life unfurling.

# Prayer stool

There it was
Gracing the footpath of a well-heeled house
In a well-heeled suburb
Amongst a stove, a rake, a dining chair
And an oversize one-eyed teddy-bear:
A prayer stool of all things
Awaiting collection by the council
On a shiny Saturday morning.
Its comical incongruity beckoned
And we found ourselves, my son and I,
Lugging it home.

What bruised hopes
Or fervent yearnings
Line the creases and hollows
Of its faded blue knee rest?
I hear the whispered recitations,
The click of beads
And the crack of ancient joints
Unbending, unending
Heads bowed, in supplication,
Or shame perhaps, or renunciation
At the high scream of innocence
Cracking and shattering
Its falling shards unveiled,
Debated and dissected on national television.

In an altered atmosphere
Bishops are paraded like common criminals,
And a cardinal is discreetly dismissed
From Rome's inner sanctum,
Falling like a puppet felled
By a rising tide of revelations
As the unmentionable becomes commonplace
And the Commission turns Inquisition
Dishing out indictments and condemnations
And no absolution.

Is this, then, the seat of intercession
And forgiveness?
Or is it rage, or horror, or something else
That flung this wooden frame
Out into a suburban street
Discarded, dilapidated
And a challenge to us all?

# Spectre

Shavings of pale wood
They seemed to me at first,
Curled, heaped, swirled
Beneath the skirting board,
One on another, spilling
In soft, pliant mounds
And then I noticed
There was a stirring
As the mound fragmented,
Came to wriggling life
Each little worm separating,
Thrashing this way and that
Its purpose, their lives, laid bare.

Repulsed, I turned away
From the spectre that arose
Unbidden, and familiar
Of our own insidious industry
Our perpetual wrigglings
And obsequious squirmings
Our careless consumption
And ability for destruction.

I turned back to face it
And the thing retreated
Fragmented, if it had ever existed,
Leaving a precious awareness
Of the need for unfashionable restraint
And of our fragile, mist-thin conscience
Yearning, despite ourselves,
To be kept alive.

# Ficus macrophylla

It was a spur-of-the-moment backward glance
But for a moment it was all I saw —
A gigantic sprawling metaphor
Blotting out the pale blue sky
Stretching upwards and out
Through olive-green drapery
Across a rustling of generations
Towards sun and sea
To the here and now.

The flesh of its trunk
Swollen with years
Sprouts drooping roots
Great locks of knotted greying hair
Moving heavily with the breeze
And mottled, lengthy, hefty arms
A tangle of whorls and curves and elbows
Rounded and hollowed with time and rain,
Hold up a vast weight, and our dreams.

And so this *Ficus macrophylla*
Matronly and majestic in equal measure
Rises above its solemn Latin label
(Attached long ago by earnest botanists)
Doesn't give a fig for it or any other word
As it speaks another language
That of century-old fortitude
Stillness, and succour.

# Election Special

Election: from the Latin *eligere*, meaning 'to pluck out or select'

He eased a slice of wholemeal
Into the silver jaws of the toaster
With an eye to the seven o'clock news
Though he wasn't quite sure
He could stomach it.

After all, he wasn't young any more
The clichés gave him cramps
The slogans, stitches
And if he wasn't careful
He'd choke on the hard crust of ideology.

As it was, he struggled to swallow
The bite-sized pieces of policy
Plucked out from portfolios
Dished up to garner votes
And the great change that wasn't happening:
Global non-warming.

But then again
He'd always taken the politicians
With a greater pinch of salt
Than he took with his fish and chips.

His toast popped up
Black as the defiant lump of coal
The PM carried in to Parliament.
It was as his wife – God rest her soul – used to say:
Yesterday's fare recycled
On tomorrow's menu
Again.

# Last stop

He was sitting at the bus stop
A neat grey figure, hands folded
Formal in his trousers, shirt and tie
And beret from another age.

He heard the scrape of shoes, the brush of trousers,
And felt the old familiar panic stir
As the crowd thickened, steps quickened
And the army marched to a single beat.

He recalled when invisibility was what he craved
As teachers saluted the new regime
Scouring every face in every classroom
For the barest hint of dissidence.

He'd had a chance and taken it
Thanks to his mother's perspicacity
It was all so far away and long ago
Such treachery, such treachery.

So many years knotting up behind him,
They'd take a lifetime to unravel as
Dressing-gowned and slippered,
He'd shuffle down his corridor.

There was nothing now left to fear
But he didn't know if he could bear
The silent onslaughts and ensuing frailty
From any more invisibility.

# The quiet assimilators

Take almost any street, in any modern city
And we are there. We are the substrata of society
Ever-present, the unseen lining, the padding in the crowd.
We carry our backgrounds
Closer than our wallets, effortlessly
Yet they inform our every step, invisibly.

Because unlike our children, if we have them,
We were not born in this country we call home
But seduced by the vast air, the swaying gums
And the freedoms they implied, we chose to come.
We bought into the Australian Dream, packaging and all,
Shook off the reassuring, cloying familial ties
Jumped through immigration hoops
Applied for visas and lingered in alien passport queues
Later sealing our legitimacy in citizenship status
And all the while, getting used to new ways
Of doing things.

We have assimilated, oh God have we assimilated
Tailoring ourselves to blend in how we dress,
Our turns of speech, its intonation, and countless other ways
Or so we let ourselves believe
(Until a chance remark, 'And where is *your* accent from?'
Undoes us in a second).

So we try just that bit harder, and
Encourage our children, if we have them, just that bit more.
The big divide, you see, never was the traditional culprits
Of language or religion (we've heard it all before),
But this: that we take nothing
For granted.

Yet a kernel of obstinance buds and grows inside us
And we feel, unaccountably and frustratingly,
Growing closer to the land we left behind
Acquiring a latent faithfulness to old ways, rituals and rhythms
Which fix themselves, like beacons in our penumbral minds,
The way we left them years, decades perhaps, ago.

And so the circle closes, leaving us
Respectable citizens of the establishment
Outside, but wavering inside
Daring, in our weaker moments, to wonder
If we ever should have come.

# In the shadows

*Nel mezzo del cammin di nostra vita*
*Mi ritrovai per una selva oscura…*

(Dante, *Inferno*, Canto I)

Crossing the park this morning
The world is still and silent and waiting.
Mist lies over the grass, the trees, the everything
As lightly as a suggestion.

I tread the curving path into the bush
With something between awe and trepidation.
A slim brown snake shudders its way across the ground,
Gone in a blink, leaving me wondering
If I had only dreamed it.

I look up at the ashen underbelly of the bridge
(Not quite the turreted beauty seen from up above
But simpler, workmanlike and more prosaic),
Home to a darker side of human nature:
The ghosts of last month's flowers laid there linger still.

The path to the creek is grey and veined by tree roots
The water is flowing cleanly and clearly, not a plastic bag in sight
And cut through by a sinuous line of stepping stones
With their petticoat of pebbles, mottled lurid green with moss.

A darkening of the foliage on the other side
Brings a parallel darkening of my thoughts
And in the shadows I see the shape of my deepest fears.
I stumble over a tree trunk, fallen, split open and bleeding sap,
Its roots jerked from the earth, a gash exposed.

Righting myself, a scratching sound tears at my thin composure
But it's only a bulbous-bodied, spindly-necked bush turkey
Picking its way up the hill. I too will rise,
Negotiate my way through the mesh of undergrowth and my life,
Catching my thoughts on brambles, tripping on memories, as
Still heavy'd by longing after all these years,
I cut between great slabs of rock, polished lustrous
And emerge, at last, panting, on a high flat path
Streaked by sunlight and dappled in hope.
The blue-grey gums, dusky as eyeshadow
Sway easily against a pale sky, yet anchored to the earth
They tether in turn my own emotions
And I hear, as if on cue, the high fluting of a bird.

I tread the last quarter home,
Vindicated, triumphant.
I have, once again, negotiated the thickets of my mind
And can finally see the little things:
Weeds thriving in dull concrete
Where spoiled orchids in suburban gardens strain to grow,
Rainwater, in silver rivulets, running off the street
Pooling in ridges between pavers
Making glistening cushions of glass
Or hanging, in balls of silver on the underside of railings,
From last night's rain.

# Acknowledgements

I gratefully acknowledge the following publications in which some of the poems collected here were first published:

*Other Terrain Journal*, Issue 5, 8 June 2018: 'Now he is here'.

*New Reader Magazine*, Vol. 1, Issue 2, 13 July 2018: 'And the nuns wore lipstick' and 'Honolulu Breakfasts'.

*Literary Yard*, 24 August 2018: 'Before the party', 'What was, 'Boston Uncommon' and 'Pine nuts at lunchtime'.

*Empathy*, September 2018 (chapbook anthology of shortlisted entries for the Australian Catholic University Poetry Prize 2018): 'Recalling Sarah'.

*Backstory Journal*, Issue 6, 15 December 2018: 'Fifty-five days'.

*Down in the Dirt: Fallen Kingdom* (Scars Publications chapbook anthology), 2 January 2019: 'A glut of words' and 'Someone else's morning'.

*The Blue Nib*, Issue 37, 15 March 2019: 'A stain the shape of Italy', 'For my cousin in Faenza', 'The flick of a lizard's tail', 'The passing of things' and 'Separateness'.

*Pink Cover Zine,* Issue 4, 6 May 2019: 'I left suitcases'.

*Other Terrain Journal*, Issue 7, 16 June 2019: 'Charlie'.

*Poetica Review 2*, Summer 2019: 'A gift for the taking'.

*The Enchanting Verses Literary Review*, 31 July 2019: 'Black box'.

*The Blue Nib*, Issue 39, 15 September 2019: 'My tapestry' and 'Between beauty and decadence'.

*Miletus International Literature Magazine*, Autumn 2019: 'Oblique angles' and 'I don't want to go back'.

*Eureka Street,* Vol. 29, No. 18, 16 September 2019: 'The quiet assimilators' and 'A journey of sorts'.

*fourWthirty*, November 2019 (anthology, Booranga Writers' Centre): 'Vermeer in Boston'.

*Australian Poetry Collaboration*, No. 31, Meuse Press, 10 November 2019: 'Bedsitter'.

*Scarlet Leaf Review,* January 2020: 'The lady on the steps', 'No room for tears' and 'Destination nowhere'.

*Live Encounters Poetry & Writing*, 1 February 2020: 'Matters of the heart', 'In defence of the slimmest of events', 'Election Special' and 'Last stop'.

*Backchannels Journal*, Edn 4, 30 March 2020: 'Be-mused'.

'In the shadows' won First Prize in the Adelaide Plains Poetry Competition 2019.

'Vermeer in Boston' was shortlisted in the Booranga Literary Prize (Poetry) 2019.

'Blessed to be here' was shortlisted in the National Writing Competition 2019.

'Prayer stool' was highly commended in Scribes Writers Poetry Competition 2019.

'Acquiescence' was commended in the Woorilla Poetry Prize 2019.

'Bedsitter' was selected to be read at Poets Call Out - Spirit of Home, Manly Art Gallery 2019.

'What was' was shortlisted for the Robert Graves Poetry Prize 2018.

'Recalling Sarah' was commended in the Australian Catholic University Poetry Prize 2018.

www.ingramcontent.com/pod-product-compliance
Lightning Source LLC
Chambersburg PA
CBHW062141100526
44589CB00014B/1645